The Romance of
COUNTRY INNS

Elizabeth Bond

TODTRI

This book was designed and produced by
TODTRI Book Publishers
P.O. Box 572,
New York, NY 10116-0572
FAX: (212) 695-6984

Printed and bound in Korea

ISBN 1-880908-53-0

Author: Elizabeth Bond

Publisher: Robert Tod
Senior Editor: Edward Douglas
Project Editor: Cynthia Sternau
Editor: Terri Hardin
Consultant: Julie Barker
Book Designer: Mark Weinberg
Typesetting: Command-O Design

PHOTO CREDITS

Photographs of the inns featured in this book have been reproduced through the
courtesy of the respective innkeepers. Additional photography was supplied by:

Bullaty, Lomeo
16, 72-73, 75 (top)
Sonja Bullaty
63
Will Faller
20, 26, 27, 28 (top & bottom), 29, 92, 100, 102, 103, 104-105, 108, 109, 111, 112 (top), 118, 119, 120-121, 126 (left),
Michael McCurry
101, 106, 107
New England Stock Photo
J. Christopher 110
Jim Schwabel 112 (bottom)
Picture Perfect
40
Eric Roth
4-5, 6, 7, 12 (left), 13, 17 (bottom), 82, 83, 84, 85, 86, 87 (top & bottom), 88-89, 90 (left), 90-91,
95 (top & bottom), 96-97, 97 (right), 98 (top & bottom), 99, 122-123, 123 (right), 124, 125, 126-127

contents

introduction

4

CHAPTER ONE

landmarks of history and culture

15

CHAPTER TWO

the soul of hospitality

55

CHAPTER THREE

lovely to look at

93

index

128

introduction

the distinctive country inn is a romantic anomaly in this age of the hotel chain, the anonymous, and the prefabricated. The country inn is a vestige—one of the last holdouts—of an era of individualism, of hand-crafted comforts, and of low-tech luxuries. Inns still operate at human scale, reflecting the personalities, tastes, and hospitality of the innkeepers. They thrive—or disappear—on their ability to make guests feel at home.

Inns were once the primary lodgings for travelers. They were of modest size and found along quiet rural roads. Travel by coach or on horseback was a long, wearying journey between destinations. Inns offered comfort and safety at the end of a day's ride. A hearty meal, a drink by the fireplace, a warm bed to sleep in, and, in the morning, the journey began anew.

The twentieth century brought faster means of transportation and these, in turn, led to the creation of highway systems—the fastest routes between two points, if not the most scenic or peaceful. Many inns, cut off from these fast new roads, closed their doors for the last time. Even those on popular thoroughfares, or at resort locations, found themselves losing to the efficient, box-shaped modern versions of the "inn." An age of classic comforts and individualized service seemed to be coming to an end.

Many inns, of course, survived the onslaught of the modern and decidedly unromantic competition, particularly if they were located at popular destinations or convenient for weekenders escaping the big city. Soon these hardy survivors were joined by others as a revival of interest in the classic country inn began to grow by leaps and bounds.

The increasing sophistication of many travelers signaled an interest in lodgings that offered something more than could be found in a typical "package tour" hotel. Country inns, with their individuality,

RIGHT: An old-fashioned sleigh ride is a very special way to see the splendid New England countryside in winter.

ABOVE: At the Pomegranate Inn in Portland, Maine,
the eclectic selection of artwork and furniture adds
a delightful element to an already whimsical setting.

FOLLOWING PAGE:
The bedrooms and suites
at The Inn at Perry Cabin
are individually decorated
havens for weary guests.

their sense of history, and their various personal touches, were a perfect alternative. Even as the long-established classics thrived, they were joined by many unique and spectacular old homes, farms, and villas newly made into inns. Some inspired innkeepers resurrected the remarkable domains of long-gone millionaires' and best-selling authors' estates, resulting in luxury lodgings that go far beyond the simple comforts of the roadside inns of old.

Inns are by their nature unique—a nature no chain could hope to emulate—and they are filled with one-of-a-kind items, from precious antiques and works of art to the innkeepers themselves. Today the average hotel or motel offers a reliable sameness the world over. With a visit to a country inn there is still the sense of adventure, of discoveries to be made, or the past revived.

But the great inns don't simply turn their backs on the modern or wallow in nostalgia. They find instead a timeless romanticism in some—now largely ignored—

BELOW: The idea of discovery lies behind the remarkable decor at the Pomegranate Inn—a visual feast for guests and owners alike.

aspects of past ages: the beauty and comfort of handmade furnishings and decorations, forgotten architectural styles, gourmet meals of home-raised meats and vegetables, and awe-inspiring views, set in the midst of pollution-free, natural expanses. It is the romance of a quieter, slower-paced world that stands in stark contrast to our own.

For some, country inns are a glimpse into the past. The structures of many inns can be centuries-old, and some merely evoke distant times, while others may have specific ties to historic events or personages. Few inns fail to grasp the allure of these associations and proudly publicize their famous visitors. Guests imbued with the appropriate sense of romance can ask for the room where Robert Louis Stevenson wrote *Treasure Island* or admire the scenery that inspired Impressionist painters such as Monet.

In some cases, modern inns have been created out of what were the private homes and vacation getaways of notable names and the famously wealthy. In such cases, the visitor gets an even rarer chance to mingle with past personages. And sometimes, as in The Point on Saranac Lake in the majestic Adirondacks, the visitor may live—for a night, anyway—in exactly the style of rustic luxury as did the original owners, the Rockefeller family.

This modern era of the deluxe country inn combines the traditionalism, the aesthetics, and the romance of the old with some of the conveniences and pleasures of the new—exotic or health-conscious gourmet meals, for example, and the finest wines from around the world. And yes, even fax machines and cable television.

It is in many ways a golden age for those who would enjoy the special pleasures of a romantic stay at a great country inn. The inns within this book are but a taste of the great experiences to come.

ABOVE: The hallway of The Inn at Perry Cabin opens onto an antique-filled foyer leading into a wealth of elegant sitting rooms.

LEFT: Every guest yearns for a home away from home, and the comfortable living room at Clifton offers just such an informal setting for the sophisticated traveler.

ABOVE: The White Barn Inn enjoys a wide-spread
reputation for excellent New England cooking, and the
focus is always on fresh seafood caught by local fishermen.

RIGHT: An exceptional oasis of hospitality in Kennebunkport, Maine, The White Barn Inn offers guests the
same special warmth that greeted travelers of long ago.

RIGHT: Classically colonial inside and out, Old Drovers Inn, first established in 1750, offers the old-fashioned hospitality of an earlier era together with the comfort of modern conveniences.

RIGHT: Classically colonial inside and out, Old Drovers Inn, first established in 1750, offers the old-fashioned hospitality of an earlier era together with the comfort of modern conveniences.

LEFT: Long-necked water birds are part of the elegant landscaping at Adair, which offers a wealth of natural vistas and wildlife for walkers and hikers, as well as nearby skiing for winter sports lovers.

CHAPTER ONE

Landmarks of history and culture

Country inns are as old as the very first traveler, who, weary to the bone, knocked on a strange door and begged shelter for the night. And whether they are ancient or new, inns are part of a more informal history, into which real history—with its great and small deeds, its heroes and villains—weaves in and out.

Inns were an integral part of Colonial America, where a lively population composed of traveling farmers, merchants, Native Americans, and French fur-trappers moved up and down the eastern coast, passing through along the New York, Connecticut, Massachusetts, and Vermont borders, as far as Quebec. One such inn, Old Drovers Inn in Dover Plains, New York, has been in service since 1750. Classically colonial, its dark-beamed tap room recalls a time when drovers brought cattle down to market along the old post roads. Light comes from candles and the hearth of the old brick fireplace, and is reflected in the clusters of hanging brass pots and pewter tankards.

In true tavern fashion, the night's menu is written in chalk on a well-used blackboard. The old drovers would certainly have felt at home with the hearty, traditional fare: cheddar cheese soup, browned turkey hash, and grilled sirloin with red onions and horseradish butter.

Compared to today's standards, Old Drovers Inn is rather small. There are just four rooms, the largest of which features antique double beds, and has an unusual, scalloped ceiling. There, a night may be spent in modern comfort, while hearkening back to the days when all of America was wilderness.

LEFT: Breakfast at Adair features hot popovers fresh from the oven, a house specialty, as well as fresh fruit and, perhaps, eggs Florentine. The teapot on the table is only one of a growing collection used to serve — and delight — guests.

NEW ENGLAND CHARM

At the northern edge of the White Mountains, a charming New England country inn offers old-fashioned hospitality and warmth together with incredible natural vistas. Adair is set on a two hundred-acre estate in Bethlehem, New Hampshire, and from this picture perfect setting Patricia and Hardy Banford, together with their daughter Nancy, continue the New England tradition of welcoming friends, old and new. The hilltop mansion, originally built in 1927, has been meticulously and lovingly restored, and offers eight elegant, comfortable bedrooms, each named after the nearby mountains. A spacious, fireplaced living room, large dining room, sun porch, and recreation room add to indoor comforts, while anyone wishing more of the great outdoors after a day's hiking or sightseeing can take advantage of the flagstone terrace and the rear yard, landscaped by Frederick Law Olmsted.

BELOW: Old houses often hold many mysteries, but this extraordinary collection of hats, found in one of the many attics at Adair, are now displayed at the head of the main staircase and available for anyone to try on.

LEFT: Glen Ellis Gorge, part of the lush countryside surrounding Adair, a romantic hideaway in New Hampshire.

LEFT: A romantic hideaway in New Hampshire, Adair is set on two hundred acres with magnificent views of the Presidential and Dalton ranges. This beautiful Connecticut River Valley Georgian Colonial Revival mansion was built in 1927, and converted to an inn in 1992.

SOUTHERN HOSPITALITY

If one is to speak of plantations and the Old South, one must of course mention the historic town of Natchez, Mississippi. There, one can find Monmouth Plantation, an inn of magnificent antebellum style. A National Historic Landmark, it sits in graceful dignity amid grounds that are a vision of azaleas, magnolias, and shady moss-draped oaks. There are twenty-five rooms and suites. These have antique lamps and priceless furnishings, and above every bed and window, seemingly endless yards of fabric have been tucked and draped and fastened with bows.

Built in 1818, Monmouth started out as a Federal-style brick structure, with none of the white columns and broad, overhanging balconies associated with the antebellum architecture of Natchez. But in 1826, John Anthony Quitman purchased the property. An upstart with hopes of taking Natchez society by storm, Quitman strove to make Monmouth a showpiece and the envy of his neighbors. By the mid–1850s, he had succeeded; the Plantation was described as "very striking . . . a castle of a house—plain and rich."

Monmouth's fortunes changed with the outbreak of the Civil War. It was ravaged by Union troops, who treated the house as both bivouac and booty. With the end of the war and Quitman's death, Monmouth lapsed into a decline from which it did not recover until 1977. The Riches, the present owners, have restored the inn to its antebellum splendor.

LEFT: An elegant secretary desk accented by antique lamps is among the noteworthy furnishings found in the twenty-five well-appointed bedrooms and suites at Monmouth.

ABOVE: The dining room at Monmouth offers a truly regal setting for a spectacular five-course meal, complete with heirloom china and antique silver.

ABOVE: A National Historic Landmark, Monmouth
Plantation represents the essence of antebellum splendor,
an estate where white columns and wide balconies overlook
broad, sweeping lawns and magnolias perfume the air.

ABOVE: Painted walls and priceless antiques grace this hallway at Monmouth. The building was restored to showpiece status in 1977, and offers southern hospitality together with unparalleled elegance.

FOLLOWING PAGE: Among the many common areas at Monmouth are this lovely parlor and the adjacent music room, where a piano and harp evoke the sedate entertainments of ages past.

LONGSTANDING ELEGANCE

On April 18, 1906, a massive earthquake, followed by a sweeping three-day fire, struck San Francisco, decimating the city in one of the most spectacular natural disasters in American history. Among the few buildings that survived the 1906 disaster was the Archbishop's Mansion, built for the Archbishop of San Francisco in 1904. Today, the Archbishop's Mansion is the most spectacular bed and breakfast in the city—a not-so-humble inn where a three-story open staircase with carved wooden columns ascends to a sixteen-foot stained-glass dome and the rooms have the feeling of a French country manor. Eighteen splendid fireplaces with carved mantles may be found scattered throughout this meticulously restored building, where high arched windows reflect the grand era of its origin, and the furnishings and decoration are a stunning blend of Belle Epoque, Victorian, and Louis XIV. Located in close proximity to the opera house and Davis Symphony Hall, the Archibishop's Mansion offers easy access to the best of San Francisco's music and art in surroundings of unparalleled elegance.

LEFT: Above the grand, three-story, open staircase is a gorgeous sixteen-foot stained glass dome, reflecting the lights of San Francisco past and present onto today's sophisticated travelers.

ABOVE: The entryway, common rooms, and hallways of the Archbishop's Mansion are decorated in French Second Empire style, and give the feeling of an elegant country manor at its finest.

LEFT: Comfort, elegance, and
an astonishing mixture of period
furnishings make this Archbishop's
Mansion bedroom a splendid
resting place for any guest.

LEFT: Cocktails at the Archbishop's
Mansion might be followed by
a night at the opera or a concert
at Davis Symphony Hall, both
located in close proximity to
these elegant surroundings.

RIGHT: San Francisco, one of
the most gracious and picturesque cities in the United States,
was almost completely rebuilt
after the 1906 earthquake.
Among the surviving buildings
was the spectacular Archbishop's
Mansion, built in 1904.

DAYS OF FEUDAL SPLENDOR

In the Old World, many of today's most delightful inns trace their origins back to the landed gentry. England's Buckland Manor, for example, has only been a country house hotel since 1982, but in its time, it has been beloved of kings, ecclesiastics, and scholars. It was mentioned in the famed Domesday Book, drawn up by William the Conqueror in the eleventh century. This alone would make the manor fairly venerable, but actually it goes back farther, to the time when knighthood was beginning to flower, and small kingdoms warred with one another for sovereignty. One such sovereign, Kynred of Mercia, gave up his crown for the religious life in A.D. 709. He divested himself of his worldly goods, which included Buckland's parcel of land, and his award of the manor to a local monastery was duly noted in the monks' books.

What is now the inn proper dates from the thirteenth century. Built of the region's honey-colored stone, the manor overlooks the romantic Cotswolds countryside. The grounds contain manicured gardens,

ABOVE: At the manor's table, the herb gardens and fruit arbors at Buckland lend a medieval presence to the traditional cuisine served in surroundings graced by antiques from many centuries.

RIGHT: Part of the rich tapestry of English history, Buckland Manor was mentioned in the Domesday Book, drawn up by William the Conqueror in the eleventh century. The buildings at Buckland in use today date from the thirteenth century, and are built from the region's honey-colored stone.

RIGHT: After a day spent
rambling through the Welsh
countryside, it's a true
pleasure to return to the
Porch at Llangoed Hall,
where all boots must
patiently wait for tomor-
row's scenic excursion.

RIGHT: The magnificent
Library at Llangoed offers
the indoor pleasures
of an Edwardian house
party to guests who want
a home away from home.

croquet lawns, and tennis courts, but also have the woodland beauty of the English countryside. Strolling past the lovely gardens, one may find oneself on the Cotswold Way, a centuries-old trail.

Outwardly, the Buckland Manor retains the aura of the middle ages with its herb gardens and fruit arbors (the products of which also grace the traditional cuisine of the manor's table) and the medieval church that still stands on the property. The manor's interior has been lovingly redecorated with antiques from many centuries, and all with an eye toward authenticity. Of its fourteen guest rooms, the Abbots Room and the Delany Suite, with their mullioned windows, are in the oldest part of the house.

When Sir Bernard Ashley's Llangoed Hall in Wales opened in 1990, the BBC threw a three-day gala event for the writers and playwrights at the Hay-on-Wye literary festival. As one guest, a famous American playwright, was leaving, he was asked if he wished to meet the hotel manager. "Oh," he replied, " I thought I was staying in somebody's home." Llangoed Hall recreates the atmosphere of an Edwardian house party with all the modern-day comforts. Time moves on, fashions change, but there is still a place in Wales where the elegance and pleasures of days gone by intersect with the needs of today's sophisticated travelers. At Llangoed, you can birdwatch, explore the shops in nearby Llyswen or Hay-on-

ABOVE: Whether it's a late breakfast of sausage and tomatoes or an elegant dinner prepared from your very own salmon freshly caught that same day in the River Wye, dining at Llangoed Hall is an experience not to be missed.

LEFT: After a pleasant day antiquing or bird watching in the countryside, a canopied four-poster bed welcomes the returning Llangoed Hall guest for a well-deserved rest.

Wye, visit the silver waterfalls of the Elan Valley, or wander through the hotel's magnificent gardens to the River Wye to join other guests fishing for salmon, while enjoying the excellent hospitality and comfort of a home away from home.

Les Templiers, which is just east of Orléans in the fertile Loire Valley, is also associated with knighthood. Les Templiers may look like a humble wayside inn, but appearances belie its noble lineage. The inn was named after its first master, Everard des Barres, who was third commander of the notorious Knights of the Temple, or Templar. These were an order of Crusaders who were first associated with the fabled Temple of Solomon, then characterized as "mystics" and freebooters. The last Master of the Temple, Jean de Molay, was tried for sorcery and burned at the stake in 1314.

The original structure, which was built in the early twelfth century, apparently shared the fate of the Templars, and was scourged from the land. The present structure, with its half-timbered façade, was built in the eighteenth century. As recent as it is, Les Templiers nonetheless strives to evoke its distant past. There is a massive beam that depicts the knights' hunting stags, and a heraldic shield worked in stone above the fireplace. The room is ringed by a minstrel gallery that is supported by huge timbers.

The Dépée family has welcomed guests to Les Templiers since 1946, and the current innkeepers, Philippe and Françoise, have created its comfortably rustic decor. There are seven thatched cottages which contain twenty-two rooms and eight suites. The inn is near the forests of Sologne, from which wild mushrooms and wild game are brought to Les Templiers' table in a variety of delicious dishes. Local fish from the Loire round out the fare, which may be accompanied by a spectacular selection of wines.

North of Stuttgart, Germany, near the town of Oehringen, stands the Wald & Schlosshotel, a royal hunting lodge that has been in the Hohenlohe-Oehringen family for almost three centuries. Its heritage is made plain as soon as one enters the Jägerstube, an informal dining room, and beholds the trophies of stags' antlers and mounted hunters' rifles.

Wald & Schlosshotel is composed of several buildings, which include a rustic, half-timbered lodge with an onion-domed tower and

RIGHT: Set in rolling fields about fifty miles outside London is historic Hartwell House, where King Louis XVIII of France once took his ease while Napoleon waged war with England.

an elegant white-stucco building with gabled roof. Built in 1712 by Prince Johann-Friedrich zu Hohenlohe-Oehringen, the Wald & Schlosshotel hearkens back to an age of comfort and visual opulence. Everywhere is deep, plush velvet, warm-toned mahogany, and the glitter of crystal chandeliers and gold objects. Some of the guest rooms have antiques and formal sitting areas; others, the relaxed charm of a country home. The inn itself is surrounded by a magnificent seven-acre park where guests may hunt the game of the season.

Over the years, the Hohenlohe-Oehringen family established a superb cellar, said to hold a thousand wines. One of these is Verrenberg, aged on the premises in oak casks that bear the family crest.

ABOVE: No humble country inn, Les Templiers takes its name from Everard des Barres, third commander of the notorious Knights Templar. Dine al fresco in the garden and admire the seven thatched cottages that house guests.

FOLLOWING PAGE: The romantic Cotswolds countryside surrounding Buckland Manor is endowed with lush woodlands and quaint stone cottages such as this.

LEFT: At Les Templiers, wild game and mushrooms from the nearby forests of Sologne appear like magic on the table, and a special selection of wines from the Loire Valley is available to tempt discerning palates.

ROYALTY AND ROBBER BARONS

Few inns can boast a royal exile, but Hartwell House can. Located about fifty miles from London, Hartwell House was once the estate of the Hampden and Lee families—the latter being the ancestors of General Robert E. Lee. But Hartwell House is best known for having entertained Louis XVIII, one of the last French monarchs.

While Napoleon was warring with the British, Louis chose to rise above the fray, lounging at Hartwell House with numerous courtiers and his dipsomaniacal mate, Marie-Josephine of Savoy. Not all was wine and roses, however; Marie-Josephine took a dislike to, of all things, the newel posts of the mansion's staircase. She called them "grotesque" and had them removed. Uneasy lies the head that wears the crown . . . .

The historic house, which dates from the seventeenth century, was restored to its splendor in 1986. It is a fairly large inn. There are thirty-one bedrooms and suites, with another sixteen guest rooms situated in the restored stable block, now called Hartwell Court. Each guest room is named for members of the Bourbon Family, to commemorate Louis XVIII's brief reign at Hartwell.

Without indigenous royalty, America has had to make do with the very rich. Some of the country houses built in the time of the Robber Barons have now been turned into dazzling and well-appointed inns. One example is Wheatleigh, a turn-of-the-century mansion nestled in the Berkshire mountains. Wheatleigh was built as a wedding present from the wealthy H. H. Cook to his daughter. And since her groom was of royal lineage, it was felt that the house also had to be of regal proportions.

LEFT: Gleaming yellow daffodils accent the carefully manicured grounds of Hartwell House, restored to its original seventeenth-century splendor in 1986.

ABOVE: Set in rolling fields about fifty miles outside London is historic Hartwell House, where King Louis XVIII of France once took his ease while Napoleon waged war with England.

ABOVE: In the King's Room at Hartwell
House, guests can experience royal
hospitality in truly historic surroundings.

ABOVE: Each of the guest rooms at Hartwell House is named after a
member of the Bourbon Family. This luxurious bedroom combines the
ample space and proportions of the past with modern ideas of comfort.

A sixteenth-century Florentine palazzo, with columns, arcades, high-ceilinged rooms, and balustrades, served as a model. Louis Comfort Tiffany created Wheatleigh's windows and lanterns, while its chandeliers were made at Waterford, Ireland. Craftsmen worked garlands of flowers, profusions of ivy, and legions of cherubs and angels into Wheatleigh's monumental fireplaces, and laid hundreds of square yards of oak into a marvelous herringbone parquetry. In spite of it all, Wheatleigh's luxury seems in perfect balance with the simple beauty of its Berkshire surroundings.

Several rooms have balconies with outstanding views, as well as working fireplaces. A duplex suite that was once an aviary became a favorite of Leonard Bernstein's, who used to book the rooms when he was conducting at the neighboring Tanglewood Music Festival.

OF ARTISTS AND WRITERS

Throughout the centuries, inns have played host to many of the great names in art, literature, music, and the theater. In most cases these have been mere brushes with greatness, lodging, and a meal given to a passing legend. In others, though, the associations have been significant ones. Some inns were the long-time residences of notable artists, and some have even been immortalized in poetry or prose or paintings by their inspired guests.

Inns with a connection to famous art and artists have had a special allure for contemporary visitors. To be able to live for a time under the same roof as a great nineteenth-century painter, perhaps sit at the same desk where a Nobel Prize winner wrote his masterpieces—these are opportunities to commune with the creative past that no museum or biography can ever match.

LEFT: Tucked away on a twenty-two acre estate in the Berkshires, Wheatleigh was built during the late 1800s in the style of a sixteenth-century Italian Renaissance palace. This magical building features Tiffany windows and lanterns, and Waterford chandeliers.

BELOW: Everything is romantic at Wheatleigh, beginning with its history. Each of the seventeen guest rooms is unique, and individually decorated in a balance of contemporary design and antiques chosen to enhance the building's spectacular architecture.

LEFT: The sweeping staircase at Wheatleigh leads to such luxurious and unusual accommodations as the Count and Countess' room, which has a dome ceiling and curved walls.

RENAISSANCE SPLENDOR

No inn has a more ancient association with an artist, nor with a more notable figure in the whole history of art, than that of the Villa San Michele with Michelangelo Buonarroti, the incomparable sculptor, painter, and architect. Michelangelo's works, from the Sistine Chapel in the Vatican to the *Pieta*, are some of the most inspired works ever created. In addition, the artist did hundreds of commissioned pieces, statues, frescoes, and architectural designs for various clients, none lacking at least a touch of genius.

A few miles outside of Florence, the city where Michelangelo was raised, the Villa San Michele rests in the hills of Fiesole. This sixteenth-century building, once a monastery, and later a convent, is classified as a National Trust monument in Italy because of the now undisputed belief that its façade was designed by the great artist himself. The Villa began taking guests in the 1950s, with gradual renovations that have brought it up to its present luxurious standards. Sightseers to an area of Italy surrounded by great works and remnants of the Renaissance can take a special thrill in the notion of a stay within walls of a Michelangelo creation.

The present owners of the Villa have cleverly retained the aura of the past, with few if any of its discomforts. The fifteenth-century antiques are polished and refined. Under the open arches on the *loggia*, with framed views of the valley, guests take their meals on warm days, and enjoy a sophisticated menu of regional Italian cuisine. The accommodations, which once were spartan monks' cells, are outfitted today with canopied beds, fine linen sheets, and rich fabrics and furnishings, and the state-of-the-art bathrooms containing whirlpool baths that would have been unrecognizable to designer Michelangelo or those ancient holy residents.

LEFT: Nestled in the hills of Fiesole, a few miles outside of Florence, is the sixteenth-century Villa San Michelle—at one time a monastery, later a convent, and now a very special Italian inn.

LEFT: South of Paris lies the
Hôtellerie du Bas-Bréau, where,
in the early nineteenth century,
artists and painters gathered
to enjoy the inspiration of the
surrounding gardens and scenery.

LEFT: Lovers of literature and
travel alike will be at ease in this
large, comfortable bedroom at
the Hôtellerie du Bas-Bréau.
It was in such as room that Robert
Louis Stevenson wrote his epic
adventure novel *Treasure Island*.

RIGHT: In 1994, The Stockton Inn
was invited to showcase its remarkable culinary talents at the James
Beard House, in New York's
Greenwich Village, assuring
further recognition as one of
Hunterdon County's most
notable dining establishments.

THE IMPRESSIONISTS

In the village of Barbizon, France, just south of Paris, at the two-centuries-old Hôtellerie du Bas-Bréau, the connection to a famous literary figure is proudly announced on the signpost. "Stevenson's House" it says, referring to Robert Louis Stevenson, who wrote much of his immortal tale of pirates and a brave boy, *Treasure Island*, within the walls of this atmospheric retreat. Today's visitors to the Bas-Bréau can specifically request the room where Stevenson stayed and worked on his most famous tale, one of the inn's most comfortable with a lovely view of the courtyard below.

The Scottish storyteller is not the only creative notable to spend time at the Bas-Bréau. Early in the nineteenth century, the town of Barbizon had become a haven for artists and painters such as Rousseau, Corot, and Millet. Beginning in 1865, the inn began exhibiting and selling the paintings of these men in order to settle some of their unpaid bills. The fresh flowers in the rooms and surrounding gardens can still inspire beautiful pictures today. The celebrated have continued to flock to the Bas-Bréau, its guest book recording the visits of such names as Princess Grace of Monaco, actor Alain Delon, and Japan's Emperor Hirohito, who took lunch at the inn.

In another part of France, Honfleur in Normandy, can be found the enchanting La Ferme Saint Siméon, an inn rich in associations with the era of the Impressionists. The quality of the light at Honfleur, the sharp-edged brightness of the landscape, and the reflective waters were a delight to a group of artists that included Monet, Boudin, and Jongkind, among others. At the inn run by "Mother" Toutain they drank the strong, homemade cider and exchanged their thoughts on this new style of painting.

Much of La Ferme Saint Siméon remains as it did in the nineteenth century and before. Indeed, the thousand-pound ceiling beams were hoisted into place some three hundred years ago. The brick and stone exterior of the farmhouse with its ivy covering evokes a time long past. Actually, some of the inn's aged, rustic aura is a carefully maintained illusion. Visitors are accorded luxurious accommodations and gourmet meals that no humble rustic inn could have afforded.

Lunches at La Ferme are an exercise in the romantic, sitting at tables under the apple trees where Monet once played dominoes and pondered his next great work, drawn from the beauty that surrounds the area.

Far way from France, in New Jersey, Broadway veterans have given a delightful New World inn its greatest distinction. Two incomparable composers of popular song, Richard Rodgers and Lorenz Hart, were inspired by their stay at The Stockton Inn, and composed the tune, "There's a Small Hotel (with a Wishing Well)" in its honor. The song was heard in Rodgers and Hart's show *On Your Toes* and has been recorded hundreds of times through the years. The Inn has maintained its old-fashioned charms (having been in operation since the 1790s) as described in the song, while adding such modern things as a gourmet restaurant and elegantly furnished rooms.

ABOVE: In season, fine-tuned palates at the Stockton Inn may feast by the waterside, an added attraction even for an inn that considers dining to be like theater—with the food as the main characters, and wine, service, and setting as supporting elements.

RIGHT: Experience the same astonishing quality of light that inspired the great Impressionist painters at La Ferme Saint Siméon, in Normandy, where Monet himself once played dominoes under the apple trees.

RIGHT: The Inn's luxurious bedrooms are furnished with English antiques, lush fabrics, and extravagantly canopied beds. After an elegant dinner, you can sip the last few drops of dessert wine in your own private sitting room.

CHAPTER TWO

the soul of hospitality

LEFT: Patrick O'Connell's cuisine at The Inn emphasizes local produce, fish, game, and wines, and each delicious meal unfolds like an intricate plot, filled with mystery and delightful surprises.

ood food is one of life's greatest satisfactions, as various writers from Epicurus and Brillat-Savarin to M. F. K. Fisher have pointed out. And while good food inspires poetry and philosophic reflection in the best of times, it quickens the heart at any time.

SIMPLY PERFECTION

The perfect country inn, one imagines, is a little out-of-the-way place, where the most extraordinary food is served to perfection. Happily, these are not unusual. Such a place is The Inn at Little Washington, Virginia. Situated near the Blue Ridge Mountains, it first began as a restaurant in 1978; in 1984, twelve guest rooms and suites were added, for the pleasure of guests wishing to stay for a respite from the modern world. The Inn was the idea of chef Patrick O'Connell and his partner, Reinhardt Lynch, both of whom studied food and service in Europe's best inns and restaurants for three years before trying their hands at innkeeping. Their dedication to excellence has made the Inn at Little Washington first and foremost renowned for its cuisine.

PREVIOUS PAGE:
Sunrise in the Blue
Ridge Mountains,
one of the East Coast's
major recreation areas.

RIGHT: Overlooking Virginia's
Blue Ridge Mountains, The
Inn at Little Washington is
both a romantic country house
hotel and a superb restaurant.

The Inn's gastronomic creations depart from the canon of classical French cuisine with unusual but excellent flourishes, employing recipes and ingredients from both old and new worlds in nontraditional ways. To begin with, foie gras is layered on top of ham and Southern-style black-eyed peas; a tangy red bell pepper soup is topped with whipped cream and Sambucca. Other magnificent inventions include local trout smoked over applewood, accompanied by a horseradish-and-apple cream sauce; and Lobster Napoleon with Golden Ossetra caviar.

A fine selection of Virginia wines is served along with dinner. The state's vineyards and wineries are a little-known industry, but they have been part of the Virginia landscape since Thomas Jefferson's day. Several varieties of chardonnay (including the Inn's own house label) and sauvignons are grown domestically by the area's forty-two vintners.

The Inn at Little Washington began as a quaint little building that had seen various incarnations as a dance hall, country store, and garage. It is now in the style of an English country manor. The rooms achieve a stateliness that does not intimidate; an eclectic decor of antiques, modern pieces, and fabrics of sumptuous colors and textures—and fresh flowers, arranged in sweet, informal bouquets—create an atmosphere of casual elegance.

Virginia boasts another gastronomic gem: L'Auberge Provençale, a French country inn that has been transplanted to this side of the Atlantic. L'Auberge Provençale is a mixture of old and new. The stone farmhouse, with its broad porch, has stood amid the pastures of northern Virginia for some 240 years, but the inn is a recent creation of owners Alain and Celeste Borel.

BELOW: At L'Auberge Provençal, fourth-generation chef Alain Borel and his wife, Celeste, have recreated French country hospitality in the tiny town of White Post, Virginia.

The rich aromas of cooking and baking that waft through L'Auberge are its premier attractions. A fourth-generation hotelier from Avignon, innkeeper Alain Borel is also a chef of note. He has prepared a showcase meal at the James Beard Foundation, and been featured in a television documentary.

Borel's menus are often planned around locally available game, which he buys from neighboring farms. The vegetables and herbs he grows himself, some from seeds brought back from France. Fifty-four fruit trees are a further extension of his pantry. He plants, tends, harvests, and chops, and soon from the kitchen come imaginative and perfectly prepared creations. Lunch and dinner may be accompanied by a carefully chosen vintage from the Borel's excellent wine cellar. Breakfast at L'Auberge is particularly memorable, and includes elegant, fruit-filled crêpes topped with crème fraîche, or scones with bits of lamb sausage and caraway tucked into the dough; there are also local shiitake mushrooms, sprinkled over thinly sliced breast of duck.

L'Auberge's wonderful *gastronomie* is set off to perfection by its delightful decor. The inn is decorated with objects that bear witness to the Borels' Provençal heritage: battered copper pots that were once Alain's great-grandmother's grace the peach-colored dining room walls; where full-length windows provide views of pastoral calm. A menagerie of hand-carved wooden animals, some made by Alain's father, has been artfully mixed together by Celeste with lively reproductions of Picasso, Matisse, and Dufy paintings.

Alain's wife Celeste has combined these French country furnishings with hand-painted Spanish tiles (used as a fireplace surround). In the guest rooms, Colonial-era

LEFT: Elaborate desserts abound at L'Auberge Provençal, and diners must remember to leave room for temptations such as gâteau angelique (chocolate soufflé cake with hazelnut praline and Frangelica cream).

ABOVE: Every meal at L'Auberge Provençal is a special occasion, and several different dining rooms offer an appropriate mood for a quiet winter dinner or cheerful breakfast.

LEFT: After a night at L'Auberge Provençal, a multi-course breakfast is served to guests, featuring home-made croissants and breakfast breads, café au lait, and, perhaps, crêpes with berries and crème fraîche.

LEFT: An elegant prix fixe dinner at L'Auberge Provençal might include smoked salmon and Beluga caviar crêpes, saddle of rabbit with cognac, foie gras, and truffles, and gâteau angelique.

RIGHT: Guests at L'Auberge Provençal can enjoy the natural beauty of the nearby Blue Ridge Mountains.

reproductions, mixed with antiques, comfortable armchairs, and unusual crafts, are employed in a delightfully inviting manner. Success has smiled on L'Auberge. When the Borels opened in 1981, they had only four guest rooms. There are now ten, as well as three dining rooms to hold the guests and others who seek to worship at the altar of fine cuisine.

Another French transplant, this time to England's shores, is Le Manoir aux Quat' Saisons, in Great Milton, England. Le Manoir has been on the lips of those in the know ever since it opened in 1984, and the reputation of Chef Raymond Blanc has compelled many a gourmand to travel to this somewhat remote country house and restaurant in the pastoral Cotswolds.

Le Manoir maintains a staff of twenty lieutenant-chefs to assist *le maître*. Needless to stay, the kitchen is a blur of brass pots and white jackets. Though not trained in the classic cuisine of France, Blanc the chef is a skilled innovator, and what emerges from the kitchen is very much a product of his own art. A typical menu might include a delicate mousse of squab liver, laced with Port wine; or monkfish, gently breaded and served with a sauce Provençal. Entrees may be simple, such as fillet of lamb roasted with rosemary; or elaborate, such as a boned leg of chicken, Bresse-style, that has been filled with a mousse and served with wild mushroom sauce.

Le Manoir is housed in a fifteenth-century manor, on an estate that dates back to Norman times. The present-day estate is beautifully landscaped on twenty-seven acres, on which can be found a romantic water garden. The rooms are splendidly furnished in rich woods with glints of gold, although some, like the Loxton dining room, reflect the informality that one associates with country living.

There are ninety staff members for the nineteen-bedroom inn, who maintain the house and the grounds, which include the gardens. In these gardens of Le Manoir sixty varieties of vegetables are grown, some of which are found nowhere else in Britain. Aubergines, artichokes (both the Jerusalem and globe variety), four types of beans, beet root, and a type of carrot called *Nantes tantes*. The herbs, lettuces, and salad greens are similarly diverse.

LEFT: The bedrooms and suites at Le Manoir aux Quat' Saisons offer a high standard of comfort and luxury. Fresh-cut flowers decorate every bedroom, and many have their own private terrace gardens.

ABOVE: Le Manoir aux Quat' Saisons is a fifteenth-century manor set on an estate that goes back to Norman times. Here, a staff of ninety tends the house and grounds of the nineteen-bedroom inn, offering unparalleled food and accommodations to discerning guests.

COUNTRY COOKING

Like Le Manoir, Ballymaloe House, in County Cork, Ireland, is known for the quality of its cuisine throughout the world. The fish for the nightly menu arrives fresh daily on the fishing boats of Ballycotton Harbor. Every vegetable and every fruit served has either been grown on the inn's own four-hundred-acre farm or on land nearby. The bread is always hot and freshly baked, and the meat is selected that day at the area's finest meat market. Ballymaloe also has a wine cellar that is considered excellent.

Ballymaloe's award-winning kitchen is presided over by the owner, Myrtle Allen; in fact, almost everyone who works at Ballymaloe was either born or married into the Allen family. Although the Allens have been serving their delicious food to the public for less than thirty years, everywhere in evidence is that timeless Irish hospitality that makes one feel welcomed as a special guest into a family home.

Though such foods as pizza may be offered, the house specializes in traditional "family" fare, such as cream soups and roasted meats of all sorts. There are also those exotics that have become staples since the days of Empire, such as curried lamb with *poppadums* (a crispy flat bread); and there are delightful deserts, such as ginger-pear upside down cake. Originally a fourteenth-century castle, Ballymaloe has been rebuilt and renovated over the centuries by its numerous owners, with only the Norman keep maintaining its original form. The house contains thirty rooms; and the gatehouse, dating from the sixteenth century, is now a two-story guest accommodation. Nearby, visitors may savor the Irish countryside and Ballycotton's quaint harbor.

Also, in the finest English tradition, the Arundell Arms has cossetted guests in the quiet little village of Lifton, England, for almost three hundred years. Originally called the White Horse Inn, it was renamed for William Arundell, a profligate who, having bought the property in 1815, went on to lose it in a snail race.

Since then, more prudent owners have built the reputation of the Arundell Arms to an almost legendary status as one of Britain's foremost

LEFT: The Old Gatehouse at Ballymaloe is a small sixteenth-century building which originally housed the guards who protected the castle entrance.

LEFT: Myrtle Allen, the owner and chef of Ballymaloe House, believes that good food and wholesome food are very close together in nature—a philosophy which has not only filled the Ballymaloe dining room but won her Michelin and Ritz awards.

BELOW: Ballymaloe House, a converted Norman castle, is acclaimed by both Irish and international food guides as a mecca for Irish country house cooking and hospitality.

sporting inns. At Arundell, the uniquely British dual heritage of the hunt and the love of the countryside is set off to perfection.

Fishing is superb. The hotel owns some twenty miles of the nearby Tamar river and its four tributaries, the Thrushel, Otterey, Lyd, and Carey. Brown trout, sea trout, and salmon abound in profusion, almost begging to be caught. In winter, hunting is the prevalent pastime, with pheasant, snipe, and red deer all particular favorites.

After enjoying the day's sport, guests may bear their prizes to Master Chef of Great Britain Philip Burgess, who prepares the trout with asparagus and a basil butter, or salmon poached to taste. If the day has not yielded a dinner-size catch, or if they are simply choosing to relax, guests can enjoy the Arms' award-winning cuisine, which is all based on local fare, such as new lamb in mint and saffron sauce, filleted duckling in an herb crust, as well as the traditional pan-fried lambs kidneys.

However sportsmanlike, the Arundell Arms has appeal for all. If one knows nothing of hunting or fishing, nearby the inn is Dartmoor, that quintessential home of fog and bogs which served as an eerie backdrop for the Sherlock Holmes classic, *The Hound of the Baskervilles*. There, along the lonely moor or at nearby Tintagel castle, one might invent one's own gothic tale.

ABOVE: "If forced to chose just one complete hotel to accompany me to my desert island . . . I suppose it would have to be Ballymaloe. It is quite simply the perfect hotel."
—*The London Observer*

TRADITIONAL CUISINE

In another tradition entirely, travelers to Italy may savor the pastoral delights of Tuscany, praised for its warm sun and gentle hills from time immemorial. From this ancient, fertile land comes some of the finest food in all the world. Rich semolina wheat, limpid olive oil, fragrant herbs, and luscious fruit—all play a part in the cuisine that has graced Tuscan tables for centuries, and whose voluptuous pleasures have recently been rediscovered by the world at large.

There one finds La Chiusa, an unpretentious inn, housed in an old stone farmhouse in the hills southeast of Siena. In its courtyard stands a wood-burning oven, where the bread is still fresh-baked each day. The oven is a perfect symbol of La Chiusa's simple nature and its focus on providing country hospitality.

From the kitchen come steaming Tuscan soups, rabbit marinated and stewed in an herbal tomato sauce, pigeon cooked with fresh sage, or baby roasted lamb rubbed with an infused rosemary oil. The menu changes daily, depending on what is available, but it is always prepared with ingredients that come from the inn's own farm or from those nearby. Whether cheese, wine, meat, olive oil, herbs, or vegetables, nothing travels more than an hour to La Chiusa's kitchen.

The innkeepers Dania and Umberto Lucherini have worked hard to make La Chiusa invitingly rustic. The restored farmhouse and barn house twelve guest rooms, each with a separate entrance. These are comfortably furnished in a country style, and most have fireplaces. The vaulted dining room is the perfect place to enjoy the pride of La Chiusa, which is the hearty Tuscan cooking of Signora Luccherini.

Outside, La Chiusa looks across a broad valley to Montepulciano, a town with memories that stretch back to the middle ages. On a warm day, one may sit at a table on La Chiusa's terrace with a fabulous meal and a glass of robust Italian wine at hand, gaze on the spectacular view, and feel that life could hold no more.

In all, the fare of the country inn, whether it be *haute cuisine* or solid

FOLLOWING PAGE: Red roses and an orange tree ripe with fruit grace the charming garden of this romantic Tuscan inn.

LEFT: Some of the finest food in the world comes from Tuscany, and meals at La Chiusa, a country inn set in a converted farmhouse southeast of Sienna, offer local produce from the surrounding hills and valleys.

ABOVE: At La Chiusa, fresh-baked bread is prepared daily in an old-fashioned wood-burning oven.

COME INTO MY HOUSE

The first innkeepers were kindly souls who opened their doors to weary travelers. In the beginning, it was simply a bowl of pottage and a pallet near the hearth; gradually, as trade grew, whole rooms were readied and meals grew more elaborate. And thus the tradition of hospitality was born. The Swag, for example, near Waynesville, North Carolina, is owned by Rev. Dan Matthews, rector of New York City's historic Trinity Church, and his wife, Deener. As with the earliest country inns, The Swag was originally meant only for family use, but became an inn when, in 1982, the Matthews began to accept a few overnight guests. They gradually converted their home until they now have sixteen guest rooms.

The inn takes its name from an Appalachian term for a dip between two mountain tops. Indeed, the Swag's hand-hewn log cabins have views that stretch fifty miles over the historic and beautiful Smoky Mountains. (Interestingly, the cabins were not originally found *in situ* but were gathered from all over the area and reassembled by design.)

The cabins' interiors are paneled with barnwood and chestnut, and have stacked-stone fireplaces. They have both elegance and a kind of amiable rusticity. The Chestnut Lodge, for example, is paneled with boards that have a medium-brown hue, and no paint or wallpaper covers the wormholes that time has wrought. The workmanship and the natural chestnut tone have the quality of silk.

The Matthews have taken care to enhance the natural beauty of their cabins with pieces of exquisite craftsmanship, and The Swag reflects this obvious love of creation. Every bed has a handmade quilt, and every

LEFT: Black bears are among the most frequently sighted animals in the forests of the Smoky Mountains.

BELOW: The Swag takes its name from an Appalachian term for a dip between two mountain tops. Guests are housed in hand-hewn log cabins overlooking the beautiful Smoky Mountains.

LEFT: Guests can happily relax in the rustic charm of the living room at The Swag.

room contains original art from Smoky Mountains artisans and others. The bedsteads themselves were created by David Robinson, whose gazebo and a rustic bridge for New York's Central Park reflect his appreciation of nature's forms. Each bedstead is fashioned out of rhododendron branches, some as thick as a flagpole. At the bed's head and foot, the branches gracefully curve to form two partial arcs, where the artist makes glorious use of the wood's natural twists and burls.

In The Swag's library, books are shelved in stacked apple crates, the top levels of which can be reached by means of a handmade white birch ladder. The ladder was crafted by a local artist, Daniel Mack, who has also taught workshops at the inn on rustic furniture making. "Rustic" meaning to the craftsman and the innkeepers, "made out of real stuff" that feels good and smells good.

While the Matthews are relatively new to the trade, others have been born into the tradition of hospitality. Among rolling hills reminiscent of the classic film *The Quiet Man*, one finds Longueville House, owned since time out of mind by the O'Callaghan family. Located on a five-hundred-acre farm, Longueville House bestrides a hill that looks down on acres of field dotted with grazing sheep. Past the sheep there are lines of mighty oaks, originally planted to replicate the battle lines of the French and English at Waterloo. Still further on lies the Blackwater River

RIGHT: Every bed at The Swag has a handmade quilt, and the rooms contain original artwork by local artisans, as well as unique wooden bedsteads created by David Robinson.

and the remains of Dromineen Castle, the ancestral home of the O'Callaghans, which had been repeatedly attacked and eventually razed by the British.

Longueville House is a stately Georgian structure, with sixteen rooms set aside for guests. These are decorated, in great-house style, in a manner that is both grand and simple, and have large, airy windows. The House's symmetry, as seen from the drive, is charmingly thrown off-center by a magnificent conservatory on one side. This conservatory serves as a dining room; on a sunny morning, one can sit there in thorough enjoyment, perhaps savoring some just-baked breads and scones. On a warm evening, one can dine here, watch the stars, and feast on cuisine that is prepared by Longueville chef and scion, William O' Callahan.

Longueville's land provides every ingredient of the House's remarkable cuisine. From raspberries to gooseberries, beets to broccoli, and chives to chervil, everything is grown in the gardens. Salmon come from the Blackwater River, which runs through the estate, and is cold-smoked over oak sawdust. Even the sausages, including the Lyon-style *sauçissons*, are prepared from Longueville lamb in the House's kitchen.

ABOVE: After an evening dining under the stars at Longueville House, overnight guests will find a hearty Irish breakfast waiting for them.

RIGHT: Longueville House, a stately Georgian building decorated in a style both grand and simple, offers guests a chance to feast on cuisine provided by the five-hundred-acre farm surrounding the inn.

A MANOR REVIVED

There are innkeepers who, though seemingly "to the manor born," as well as born on the manor, are actually recent arrivals. Peter Herbert, for example, has been the "Lord" of Gravetye since 1958, when he purchased the historic manor. Now almost seventy, he is a yachtsman, game fisherman, a former oboist—and a premier innkeeper of exacting standards.

Built in 1598, Gravetye Manor is set on thirty acres and surrounded by a thousand acres of forest. The manor's gardens were designed by William Robinson, the pioneer of the English informal garden, who lived there until 1935. These once-glorious gardens had languished until the time of Mr. Herbert's purchase, and had crossed the fine line between informal and wild and weedy. Mr. Herbert promptly unearthed Robinson's original plans for the grounds and had the gardens restored to their original grandeur.

The rooms at Gravetye are meticulously maintained and their historic origins preserved. The

ABOVE: Gravetye Manor, built in 1598, is set on thirty
acres and surrounded by a thousand acres of forest.
These wonderful gardens were designed by William
Robinson, pioneer of the informal English garden.

ground floor is dark-paneled, with a baronial air; in the room named "Ash," the paneling is four hundred years old. There are enormous fireplaces, one of which bears the initials of the original owners, Katharine and Richard Infield, carved in stone. The dining room is exquisite, with its warm wood paneling and molded ceiling, and serves as a temple in which the best of English cooking and French cuisine is brought together.

The vegetables for Gravetye's meals come from its own garden, which is tirelessly cultivated. Trout comes from Gravetye's fishing pond, and salmon is smoked by Gravetye's kitchen.

The atmosphere of Gravetye is distinctly formal. This is the wish of the owner, and this is what Gravetye's guests are looking for. Because everything about the manor—the food, the service, the grounds, and the decor—is impeccable, Graveteye is immensely popular. For this reason, guests seem to find it pleasant that they themselves are held to a higher standard.

ABOVE: Everything at Gravetye Manor is impeccable, and the formal atmosphere—undertaken by inn staff and guests alike—puts extra polish on already exceptional circumstances.

CITY LIGHTS

Combining the warmth of a private residence with the privileges of a private club, the Inn at Harvard is located in the heart of Harvard Square, right next to Harvard Yard and the University's famous museums, libraries, and theaters. A contemporary Georgian-style building designed by architect Graham Gund, The Inn at Harvard opened in 1990, providing a well-received oasis of serenity in the midst of bustling Cambridge.

At the heart of The Inn is a towering four-story atrium/living room, with a pitched glass roof and cream-colored, marbleized walls. Furnished with custom-made and antique pieces, chess tables, and comfortable reading nooks, and overlooked by the windows and hallways of the guest rooms, this delightful space is much like a Venetian piazza or an old-fashioned town square. What better place to dine by candlelight and soft classical music than at the tables arranged along the library wall, or to breakfast on your own balcony overlooking the area below? Here, nothing is rushed, and guests find time to savor the evening and the culinary creations which combine the best of the classic and the exotic, such as a dried cherry and goat cheese tartlet or venison on a bed of spätzle with jalepeño jelly.

LEFT: Dinner at The Inn at Harvard is served next to the library, in a special area of the four-story, glass-roofed atrium. Here, executive chef Susan Connors displays one of her inventive dishes.

ABOVE: A selection of the culinary delights to be found at The Inn at Harvard, which serves a cuisine combining the exotic and the traditional.

ABOVE: Much like an old-fashioned village square,
the central living room/atrium of The Inn at
Harvard is overlooked by guest rooms and hallways.

ABOVE: Breakfast at The Inn at Harvard may
be taken on a private balcony overlooking the
atrium, or in the comfortable dining area below.

ABOVE: The romantic Inn
at Sawmill Farm is a
Vermont farmhouse trans-
formed into an elegant
hideaway by innkeepers
Ione and Rodney Williams.

COUNTRY QUIET

Not too far from the busy crowds of Boston is The Inn at Saw Mill Farm, quietly situated in the village of West Dover, Vermont. One of the twelve most perfect hideaways
in the world, The Inn is noted for its warmth and courtesy, and guests immediately feel
at home in this re-creation of an old barn, where hand-hewn posts, beams, and weathered boards hark back to an earlier era. The superb dining room offers country elegance and an American-continental menu with an international reputation and a
four-star rating. In 1992, innkeeper-chef Brill Williams' 36,000-bottle wine cellar won
the prestigious "Grand Award" from the *Wine Spectator* magazine. Guests may choose
from as many as nine hundred different vintages to accompany such tempting dishes
as roast duck au poivre vert, breast of pheasant-forestiere sauce, or scallopini of veal
Marsala with eggplant-cheese crepe. For outdoor sports fans, cold weather offers
downhill and cross country skiing, ice skating, and snow shoe hikes; summer delights
the less active guest with trout fishing, antiquing and the famous Marlboro Music
Festival. In any season, The Inn at Sawmill Farm offers old-fashioned hospitality in a
tranquil and congenial setting lovingly orchestrated by long-time innkeepers Ione and
Rodney Williams.

LEFT: In this re-creation of an old barn at The Inn at Sawmill Farm, hand-hewn posts, beams, and weathered boards offer evidence of an earlier era.

LEFT: The Inn at Sawmill Farm has an award-winning wine cellar with 36,000 tempera-ture-controlled bottles.

FOLLOWING PAGE: A delectable selection of deserts specially created for the guests at The Inn at Sawmill Farm.

ABOVE: At The White Barn Inn in
Kennebunkport, Maine, a century-old
tradition of hospitality awaits each guest.

RIGHT: Feast on chargrilled native
salmon or oven-roasted quail in a warm,
convivial setting at The White Barn Inn.

RIGHT: A rustic bedroom at The Point, originally one of the "Great Camps" built by the millionaires of the late 1800s, and a former vacation home of the Rockefeller family.

CHAPTER THREE

Lovely to Look at

the dictionary's description of an inn is "a building that offers food and lodging." But inns would all be rather drab spots and hardly worth writing about if they were no more than this functional definition. It is the human imagination of the innkeepers and their support system of creative architects, designers, decorators, and assorted craftsmen and artists that are responsible for the world's many unique and beautiful inns, transforming them into something more than buildings in which to sleep and eat.

While many inns attract visitors because of their proximity to notable landmarks and other sights, some others are so unusual and appealing in their architecture and decor that they are in themselves a draw for the traveler.

This allure may be in the design of the inn, representing a thriving example of a past school or era of architecture—Renaissance, Art Nouveau, American Colonial, and so on. Or it may be the interior design that gives an inn its distinction, luxurious furnishings, or the unusual antiques and decorations that fill its rooms. These are the inns that provide, for the traveler, a "sightseeing" tour of one sort or another on their very own grounds.

LEFT: This extraordinary bathroom at the Gingerbread Mansion in Ferndale, California, offers guests sybaritic luxury in a garden-like setting.

WATERING HOLES OF THE WEALTHY

The Point, on New York's Saranac Lake, is such a place. Located in the lush wilderness of the ancient Adirondack mountain range, it is one of the "Great Camps" built by the millionaires of the late 1800s, this one in particular being a vacation home of the Rockefellers. The Point was designed to seem rustic, but the sort of rusticity befitting folks who owned a good portion of the world. Massive logs and gigantic stone fireplaces, luxurious antique furnishings, the finest wines and liquors, gourmet meals fit for the finest big city restaurant. And at every window and deck, glimpses of the paradisiacal lake and forest, trees glowing gold in long, late summer sunsets.

The Rockefellers no longer own The Point, and it is now possible for others to partake of all of its rustic luxury for only a modest fortune. The money may be considered well spent for a glimpse of life lived at its finest.

BELOW: Skiers enjoying the trails at Sugarbush Mountain, the No. 1 ski resort in the East, located in Vermont's historic Mad River Valley.

LANDS FAIR AND GREEN

Many distinctive inns are far from the glamor of civilization, and Vermont—New England very much like it was a hundred or more years ago—holds many such wonderful places to escape to. The pace of things has never quite moved into a "fast track" as in other American states, leaving much of this state a place of quiet villages, centuries-old houses, aged farms, and rolling green hills and forests—or carpets of picturesque white snow in winter.

Sugarbush is a four-season hideaway set high in the Green Mountains of Vermont, where New England charm (and hospitality) caters to couples and families alike. The centerpiece of Vermont's most historic and scenic regions, the Mad River Valley, Sugarbush offers some the finest skiing on the East Coast, together with cozy mountain accommodations and superb service. Relax in the library or by the fireplace with a mug of hot mulled cider, and make sure you include a stroll to the Willow Pond outside. Take an enchanting trip through the winter snow, or challenge yourself on a eighteen-hole golf course in the summer's greenery. Everywhere, nature's beauty is reflected in the spectacular surroundings, and enjoyment is heightened by the comfortable surroundings and fine food available when you return to your lodgings at the end of the day.

ABOVE: The Sugarbush Inn, nestled between the Green Mountain National Forest and the Mad River, is the centerpiece of one of Vermont's most scenic regions.

LEFT: Fine dining is a part of the Sugarbush tradition, whether it's hot spiced cider in front of a crackling fire or a formal dinner for two.

THE GREAT OUTDOORS

The classic inns operating today have by their nature tended to avoid the hurly-burly of the overpopulated city, the noise, and pollution of the busy highway. They are most often found close to the quieter, forgotten byways, the unspoiled realms where things remain much as they have always been, and nature still looks as it was intended to look.

For many people a stay at an inn seems to go hand in hand with an appreciation of the natural surroundings. It is not surprising perhaps that almost anywhere one can go to enjoy nature at its most pristine, spectacular, or romantic, one can find nearby a complementary inn. In rarer cases, these lodgings work in such close harmony with the world around them that the sense of place is heightened to the level of the sublime. A stay at one of these may forever confirm the notion that no large hotel, however luxurious or creative, can quite compete with the well-conceived and perfectly located inn.

The Inn at Weathersfield is one of New England's great undiscovered treasures. Set on twenty-one peaceful acres in the heart of Vermont's finest recreation area, The Inn offers twelve guest rooms and suites, all with working wood-burning fireplaces. Venture forth from these creature comforts to explore the

LEFT: The fine dining room of The Inn at Weathersfield, a two-hundred-year-old Colonial inn.

ABOVE: All the well-appointed bedrooms at The Inn at Weathersfield have working wood-burning fireplaces.

LEFT: Long ago, when Vermont was part of the British Empire, local revolutionaries known as "The Green Mountain Boys" met at the Marsh Tavern to discuss their plans for an independent America. Today, the Marsh Tavern is an inn known as The Equinox.

LEFT: Featuring fine food and wine set in a grand country ambience, dining at The Equinox is always an elegant occasion.

many little towns and villages in the surrounding area, watch hand-blown glass being made in a restored mill, see how cheese and maple syrup are made, shop in quaint country stores, and tour a working farm in a Christmas card community where four of Paul Revere's church bells still ring.

MEETING PLACE OF
THE "GREEN MOUNTAIN BOYS"

Another notable historic establishment is The Equinox, a 2,300 acre, four-star resort nestled in the spectacular Green Mountains in Manchester Village, Vermont. Back in the days when Vermont was in the British Empire, local revolutionaries known as the "Green Mountain Boys" met to discuss their ideas about a new and independent America at what was then called the Marsh Tavern. Today, the old Marsh Tavern hosts its guests under the name of The Equinox.

Whether arranging for a sleigh ride or getting directions to the perfect fishing stream and hiking trail, the staff at The Equinox is dedicated to helping you explore and enjoy the magnificent Vermont outdoors. Sophisticated and experienced travelers and adventurers have found that after a day or two in the open air, fine food and drink take on an entirely different flavor. It's a true pleasure, then, to dine at The Equinox's four-star restaurant, the Colonnade, where every dinner is served in a grand country house ambience.

BELOW: Guests enjoying a sleigh ride at The Equinox, a 2,300-acre, four-star establishment in the spectacular Green Mountains of Vermont.

A CITY IN THE COUNTRY

In the celebrated Sonoma wine country one can often find city sophistication and elegance among the beauty of the vines. Madrona Manor's cuisine matches the lushness of its surroundings, and this charming Victorian retreat, originally built in 1881 as a vacation home for a wealthy businessman, has an absolutely fabulous kitchen. At Madrona Manor, homey elegance is the operating philosophy, and comfort mingles with amenities and antique furnishings in luxurious rooms with fireplaces or private decks. Part of the estate is filled with flower gardens and a citrus grove, and fresh-picked flowers such as foxglove and zinnias find their way to the guest rooms. What a pleasant way to take in the countryside!

Much more astonishing than the surrounding countryside is Morey Mansion, in Redlands, California, which presents an extraordinary compendium of archi-

tectural styles, from a Russian Orthodox onion dome to a two-story tower with a French mansard roof. The building was created, inside and out, in the late nineteenth century by shipbuilder and master craftsman David Morey as a monument of love for his wife. Inside Morey Mansion, the elegance is unparalleled, and much of the extraordinary original carved furnishings remain. The circular bay living room contains a working grand player piano.

ABOVE: At Madrona Manor, homey elegance is the operating philosophy, and comfort mingles with luxurious amenities and antique decor.

RIGHT: Madrona Manor, originally built in 1881 as a vacation home for a wealthy businessman, is a Victorian retreat with a fabulous kitchen.

ABOVE: The exterior of Morey Mansion presents an extraordinary compendium of architectural styles, from a Russian Orthodox onion dome to a two-story tower with a French mansard roof.

FOLLOWING PAGE: A bedroom at the Blackthorne Inn, Inverness, California. The multiple-level Blackthorne offers guests hot tubs in which to relax after a day spent at the near-by Point Reyes National Seashore.

LEFT: Inside Morey Mansion the elegance is unparalleled, and much of the extraordinary original carved furnishings remain—created in the late nineteenth century by shipbuilder and craftsman David Morey as a momument of love for his wife.

REACHING TO THE SKIES ABOVE

St. Orres, an inn dreamed up by an American builder named Eric Black, is located in Gualala, California, a tiny oceanside settlement three hours north of San Francisco. The town's primary landmark, St. Orres reaches to the skies with its exotic onion domes; the structure is an enthusiast's interpretation of Mother Russia on the California coastline.

Eric Black moved to Gualala (a Pomo Indian word for "water coming down place") in 1971, nursing a dream of establishing a commune where the residents would design and produce toys. (Gualala, it should be said, is a part of the world that draws its fair share of dreamers, many of whom have come to the picturesque little town looking for the simplicity and serenity of another time.) When the commune he envisioned failed to materialize, Black determined instead to build a distinctive inn, one that would reflect both the serene ideals of the town, and employed some architectural flourishes influenced by the Russian fur traders and trappers who unofficially colonized the seaport in the 1800s.

With little money for materials, Black used timber salvaged from a hundred-year-old sawmill and scrap paneling from a motel and service station. The copper domes contain metal from reject computer circuit boards. From such a grab-bag of ingredients, Black

LEFT: The dining room at St. Orres is set in a three-story dome with stained-glass windows and painted friezes along the high walls.

ABOVE: Perched on the coastline near Gualala, California, St. Orres has the remarkable exterior of a nineteenth-century Russian dacha.

ABOVE: The Alamo Square Inn in San Francisco offers a unique blend
of southern hospitality and fine European service. This period building
is a magnificent blend of Queen Anne and Neoclassical Revival styles.

ABOVE: The large, elegant parlors at the
Alamo Square Inn are well-appointed, with a
mixture of Victorian and oriental furnishings.

produced remarkable results; like Bailiffscourt, it became another recent creation that had the look of some carefully maintained relic of a more colorful past.

Guest accommodations now spread out to a series of distinctive cottages, where each portion of St. Orres is bathed in Pacific light and glowing with the warmth of its brilliantly revived timbers. Views of towering evergreens and pounding surf from private decks and crackling fires add to the generally enchanted atmosphere of this romantic inn.

MOUNTAINS MAJESTIC

Along the lip of the Continental United States where it touches the Pacific waters, one finds many special inns where some of civilization's more luxurious touches have been added to nature's magnificence in a combination that most find irresistible. Most people who used to travel to Big Sur came for the

scenery, and then passed on through. It is a truly spectacular coastline with beautiful vistas of sea and shore. Waves can be seen breaking with mesmerizing force from vantage points on the cliffs as high as a thousand feet up.

The Old Milano Inn, built in 1905, offers spectacular views of the Pacific Ocean, and six very special guest rooms are furnished with armoires and curious, elaborate beds. Stones from nearby beaches have been used to build the fireplace, and local wines abound at Old Milano's fine table.

LEFT: The beautiful Big Sur coastline inspired travelers with the spirit of the land and ocean long before the first inns were built in the vicinity.

ABOVE: This elaborate bed at the Old Milano Hotel in Gualala, California, was used as a prop in the movie *Wuthering Heights*.

LEFT: Old world elegance
and Victorian accents have
made the parlor of The
Inn, San Francisco into
a peaceful and pleasant
resting place for weary guests.

LEFT: A romantic sunset on
the Pacific Ocean at Pfeiffer
Beach, Big Sur, California.

RIGHT: English country house
charms prevails in the Snooker
Room of The Inn at Perry Cabin.

THE ROMANCE OF THE COAST

The romantic spirit of Laura Ashley, the internationally famous fashion designer and decorator who died in 1985, is a presiding inspiration at The Inn at Perry Cabin, located at St. Michaels, Maryland on the Chesapeake Bay. At Perry Cabin, Ashley's traditional British country stylings are everywhere apparent, in the inn's bedspreads, curtains, upholstery, and elsewhere, a beautiful testament to her taste and talent.

The Inn is a tribute to her memory by her husband and business partner, Sir Bernard Ashley. After Laura's death, Ashley reduced his interest in the textile industry where he had made his name, and decided to open a chain of hotels and inns in America with some of the spirit of Laura and the British country inns he admired. Sir Bernard bought an historic property, Perry Cabin, built at the time of the War of 1812 by the aide-de-camp of Commodore Oliver Hazard Perry, one Samuel Hambleton (Purser). The name of the inn derives from the fact that the north wing of the manor house was designed to resemble the Commodore's cabin on the flagship *Niagra*.

When Sir Bernard saw the inn for the first time he knew it could be his own perfect "flagship" for his planned Ashley House Hotels in America. With Perry Cabin, he set out to create a style of hospitality that would be casual in the American manner but with the best elements of an English country house, where-in much of the enjoyment of a stay comes from feeling like a friend of the host, and where the house itself

never feels ostentatious but is incidentally grand enough to have such things as a separate library, drawing room, and snooker room.

On the Miles River, just at its entry into the Chesapeake Bay, the Inn's twenty-five-acre waterfront estate is idyllic. From indoors, guests can catch glimpses of swans, flower beds, and shade trees, all visible from the Inn's French doors and dormer windows.

When the inn opened in 1990, its decor reflected the classic Laura Ashley product line—delicately patterned papers and textiles, curtains, armchairs, tablecloths, and bedspreads mixed with European antiques. No wall covering is repeated anywhere in the inn; each of the forty-one guest rooms has an individual look. This decor, along with the Inn's Oriental carpets, porcelains, and leather bound books, is in perfect tune with the Chesapeake Bay area, whose beauty and weather is often compared to an English coastal town.

ABOVE: The yacht club atmosphere of The Inn at Perry Cabin offers a safe, comfortable haven for boats and guests—sailors and landlubbers alike.

LEFT: The Inn at Perry Cabin presents the unique luxuries of an English country house— married to the warm informality of American hospitality at its best.

LEFT: When dining in the Conservatory of The Inn at Perry Cabin, try the Silver Oak Cabernet Sauvignon from Alexander Valley in Napa, California.

AT HOME IN VIRGINIA

Keswick Hall, another fine establishment lovingly created by Sir Bernard Ashley, offers a calm center in the midst of a busy world. Charlottesville's own Thomas Jefferson would have approved of Keswick, a spectacular antebellum mansion converted into a world class country house hotel. From Keswick, it's an easy journey by car to more than a dozen Virginia wineries, all of whom welcome guests, and love to fete wine lovers at special events and harvest festivals as well. Jean-François Legault, Keswick's Food and Beverage Manager, believes in good, simple cuisine, "leaving the product whole, and combining the ingredients just so." Local specialties, such as Summerfield veal, fresh quail eggs, and seasonal vegetables, are among the offerings on Keswick's fine tables, which have a wide following among guests and locals alike. Here is a place where it is possible to enjoy all the amenities of life in the comfort of "home," in true Bernard Ashley style.

LEFT: The Augusta Suite at Keswick Hall is a beautiful example of English luxury set in antebellum splendor.

RIGHT: At Keswick Hall, guests are nourished by luxuries large and small— a drink delivered by the butler along with a first edition, or a friendly game in the Card Room.

LEFT: Keswick Hall, set in the old-fashioned, tranquil beauty of Jefferson's Virginia, provides a calm center in the storm of the modern world.

ABOVE: The Carl Larsson Room at the Old
World Inn in Napa, California, is a welcome
oasis after a wonderful evening of British
hospitality from owners Janet and Geoffrey Villiers.

ABOVE: The Orchard Room at the Apple Lane Inn in Aptos, California, is decorated in a casual country style, and guests will find a polished apple next to their pillow when they retire for the night.

FOLLOWING PAGE:
The owners of Hanford House, in Sutter Creek, California, host an annual teddy bear and antique doll convention, and their collecting interests are reflected in the objects adorning their nine-room inn.

POSTMODERN, IN PORTLAND

The exotic and the daring combine in the furnishings and fixtures at the Pomegranate Inn, in Portland, Maine, where contemporary art of all types fills the guest rooms and common areas of this most whimsical establishment. Isabel and Alan Smiles moved to Portland in 1985 to open their inn. An interior designer, Isabel had been a partner in an antique shop, and her husband Alan, a member of the family's textile business, found himself greatly enjoying his time in the kitchen. What more perfect way could they have found to marry their exceptional skills than in the Pomegranate Inn, where an English garden statue holding their namesake fruit greets guests upon their entrance? Comfort is not lacking along with whimsy, and the specialties of the house keep guests returning year after year for a repeat experience.

And so our journey ends, and with visions of four-poster beds and scenic countrysides, sleigh rides and vineyards, sleek sophistication and country charm, both in Europe and in America, we have traveled far and wide to reach the heart of the country inn, wherein lies the essence and everlasting spirit of comfort and elegance.

LEFT: Artwork by contemporary artists is scattered throughout the Pomegranate in an extraordinary collection ranging from sculpture and intaglio prints to surrealist paintings.

ABOVE: The Italianate Colonial Revival Pomegranate Inn, built in 1884, is on the historic register of buildings in Portland, Maine.

ABOVE: In the entrance hall of the Pomegranate
Inn, a whimsical English garden sculpture holds
the Inn's namesake fruit in her outstretched hand.

ABOVE: Romance at the Pomegranate Inn
lies in the exotic and the daring—yet the
bedrooms are very comfortably appointed.

ABOVE: One of the unique bedrooms at
The Pomegranate Inn, where styles range
from flamboyant floral to country classic.

RIGHT: This day bed in one of the Pomegranate
Inn's luxurious bathrooms reflects the delightful
mixture of eclectic objects and attention to
creature comfort typical of the establishment.

index

Page numbers in **bold-face** type
indicate photo captions.

Adair, Bethlehem, New Hampshire, 15, 17, 17, 19
Alamo Square Inn, San Francisco, California,
    108, 109
Allen, Myrtle, 67
Apple Lane Inn, Aptos, California, 119
Archbishop's Mansion, San Francisco,
    California, 27, **27**, 28
Arundell, William, 67
Arundell Arms, Lifton, England, 67–69
Ashley, Laura, 113
Ashley, Sir Bernard, 33, 113, 117
Ashley House Hotels, 113

Ballycotton Harbor, County Cork, Ireland, 67
Ballymaloe House, County Cork, Ireland,
    67, **67**, **68**, **69**
Banford, Nancy, 17
Banford, Patricia and Hardy, 17
Barbizon, France, 51
Belle Epoque style, 27
Bernstein, Leonard, 47
Big Sur, California, 111, **111**
Black, Eric, 107
Blackthorne Inn, Inverness, California, **103**
Blackwater River, Ireland, 76–78
Blanc, Raymond, 64
Blue Ridge Mountains, Virginia, 58, 62
Borel, Alain, 59, 61
Borel, Celeste, 59
Boudin, Eugene, 51
Buckland Manor, England, 30–33, **30**, **39**
Burgess, Philip, 69

California:
    Alamo Square Inn, **108**, 109
    Apple Lane Inn, 119
    Archbishop's Mansion, 27, **27**, 28
    Blackthorne Inn, **103**
    Gingerbread Mansion, **93**
    Hanford House, 119
    Inn, The, **112**
    Madrona Manor, 100, **100**
    Morey Mansion, 100, **103**
    Old Milano Inn, 111, **111**
    Old World Inn, **118**
    St. Orres, 107–11, **107**
Carey river, England, 69
Civil War, 21
Colonial America, 15
Colonnade (Equinox restaurant), 99
Connors, Susan, **83**
Cook, H. H., 43
Corot, Jean-Baptiste Camille, 51
Cotswolds, England, 30, **39**, 64
Cotswold Way, England, 33
Dartmoor, England, 69
Davis Symphony Hall, San Francisco,
    California, 27, **28**
Delon, Alain, 51
de Molay, Jean, 36
Dépée, Philippe and Françoise, 36
des Barres, Everard, 36
Domesday Book, 30
Dromineen Castle, Ireland, 78

Elan Valley, Wales, 36
England:
    Arundell Arms, 67–69
    Buckland Manor, 30–33, **30**, **39**
    Gravetye Manor, 80–81, **80**, **81**
    Hartwell House, 36, 43, **43**, **44**, **45**
    Le Manoir aux Quat' Saisons, 64, **64**, **65**
English country house style, 113–14, **115**
Equinox, The, Manchester Village, Vermont,
    98, 99, **99**

France:
    Hôtellerie du Bas-Bréau, **50**, 51–52
    La Ferme Saint Siméon, 51, **52**
    Les Templiers, 36, **39**
French Second Empire style, 27

Georgian Colonial Revival style, **19**
Georgian style, 78
    contemporary, **83**
Germany:
    Wald & Schlosshotel, 36–39
Gingerbread Mansion, Ferndale, California, **93**
Glen Ellis Gorge, New Hampshire, 17
Grace, Princess, of Monaco, 51
Gravetye Manor, England, 80–81, **80**, **81**
Green Mountain Boys, 99
Green Mountains, Vermont, **99**
Gund, Graham, 83

Hambleton (Purser), Samuel, 113
Hampden family, 43
Hanford House, Sutter Creek, California, **119**
Hart, Lorenz, 52
Hartwell Court (Hartwell House), England, 43
Hartwell House, England, 36, 43, **43**, **44**, **45**
Hay-on-Wye, Wales, 33–36
    literary festival, 33
Herbert, Peter, 80
Hirohito, Emperor, 51
Hohenlohe-Oehringen, Prince Johann-
    Friedrich zu, 39
Hohenlohe-Oehringen family, 36
Hôtellerie du Bas-Bréau, Barbizon, France,
    50, 51–52
Infield, Katharine and Richard, 81
Inn, The, Little Washington, Virginia, 55–59,
    55, **58**
Inn, The, San Francisco, California, **112**
Inn at Harvard, Cambridge, Massachusetts,
    83, **83**, **84**, **85**
Inn at Perry Cabin, The, St. Michaels,
    Maryland, 7, 11, **112**, 113–14, **114**, **115**
Inn at Saw Mill Farm, The, West Dover,
    Vermont, 86, **86**, **87**
Inn at Weathersfield, Vermont, 97–99, **97**
inns, renewed interest in, 4–11
Ireland:
    Ballymaloe House, 67, **67**, **68**, **69**
    Longueville House, 76–78, **78**
Italianate Colonial Revival style, 123
Italian Renaissance palace style, 47
Italy:
    La Chiusa, 71, **71**
    Villa San Michele, 49, **49**

Jongkind, Johan Barthold, 51

Keswick Hall, Charlottesville, Virginia,
    117, **117**
Knights of the Temple, 36
Kynred of Mercia, 30

La Chiusa, Tuscany, Italy, 71, **71**
La Ferme Saint Siméon, Honfleur, Normandy,
    France, 51, **52**
L'Auberge Provençale, White Post, Virginia,
    59–64, **59**, **61**, **62**
Lee, Robert E., 43
Lee family, 43
Legault, Jean-François, 117
Le Manoir aux Quat' Saisons, Great Milton,
    England, 64, **64**, **65**
Les Templiers, Loire Valley, France, 36, **39**
Llangoed Hall, Wales, 32, 33–36, **33**, **35**
Llyswen, Wales, 33
Longueville House, Ireland, 76–78, **78**
Louis XIV style, 27
Louis XVIII, 43
Lucherini, Dania and Umberto, 71
Lyd river, England, 69
Lynch, Reinhardt, 55

Mack, Daniel, 76
Mad River Valley, Vermont, 94, 95
Madrona Manor, Sonoma Valley, California,
    100, **100**
Maine:
    Pomegranate Inn, 6, 7, 123, **123**, **124**, **125**, **126**
    White Barn Inn, The, **12**, **90**
Marie-Josephine of Savoy, 43
Marlboro Music Festival, Vermont, 86
Marsh Tavern (The Equinox), **98**, 99
Maryland:
    Inn at Perry Cabin, The, 7, 11, **112**, 113–14,
        114, **115**
Massachusetts:
    Inn at Harvard, 83, **83**, **84**, **85**
    Wheatleigh, 43–47, **47**
Matthews, Dan and Deener, 75
Michelangelo Buonarroti, 49
Miles River, Chesapeake Bay, Maryland, 114
Millet, Jean François, 51
Mississippi:
    Monmouth Plantation, 21, **21**, **22**, **23**
Monet, Claude, 51
Monmouth Plantation, Natchez, Mississippi,
    21, **21**, **22**, **23**
Montepulciano, Italy, 71
Morey, David, 100
Morey Mansion, Redlands, California, 100, **103**
"Mother" Toutain, 51

Natchez, Mississippi, 21
Neoclassical Revival style, **108**
New Hampshire:
    Adair, 15, 17, **17**, **19**
New Jersey:
    Stockton Inn, **50**, 52, **52**
New York:
    Old Drovers Inn, 15–17, **15**
    Point, The, 11, 93–94, **93**
North Carolina:
    Swag, The, 75–76, **75**

O'Callaghan, William, 78
O'Callaghan family, 76
O'Connell, Patrick, 55
Old Drovers Inn, Dover Plains, New York,
    15–17, **15**
Old Milano Inn, Gualala, California, 111, **111**
Old World Inn, Napa, California, **118**
Olmsted, Frederick Law, 17
On Your Toes, 52
Otterey river, England, 69

Perry, Oliver Hazard, 113
Pfeiffer Beach, Big Sur, California, **112**
Point, The, Saranac Lake, New York, 11, 93–94, **93**
Point Reyes National Seashore, California, 103
Pomegranate Inn, Portland, Maine, 6, 7, 123, **123**,
    124, **125**, **126**

Queen Anne style, **108**
Quitman, John Anthony, 21

Rich family, 21
River Wye, Wales, 36
Robinson, David, 76
Robinson, William, 80
Rockefeller family, 11, 94
Rodgers, Richard, 52
Rousseau, Henri, 51
Russian Orthodox onion dome style, 100, **101**,
    107, **107**, 111

St. Orres, Gualala, California, 107–11, **107**
San Francisco, California:
    Alamo Square Inn, **108**, 109
    Archbishop's Mansion, 27, **27**, 28
    Inn, The, **112**
    1906 earthquake, 27
sleigh ride, New England countryside, **4**
Smiles, Isabel and Alan, 123
Smoky Mountains, North Carolina, 75
Stevenson, Robert Louis, 51
Stockton Inn, Hunterdon County, New Jersey, **50**,
    52, **52**
Sugarbush Inn, Vermont, 95, **95**
Sugarbush Mountain, Vermont, 94
Swag, The, Waynesville, North Carolina, 75–76, **75**

Tamar river, England, 69
Tanglewood Music Festival, Berkshire Mountains,
    Massachusetts, 47
Thrushel river, England, 69
Tiffany, Louis Comfort, 47
Tintagel Castle, England, 69
Tuscany, Italy, 71

Vermont:
    Equinox, The, **98**, 99, **99**
    Inn at Saw Mill Farm, The, 86, **86**, **87**
    Inn at Weathersfield, 97–99, **97**
    Sugarbush Inn, 95, **95**
Verrenberg wine, 39
Victorian style, 27, 100, 109, **112**
Villa San Michele, Fiesole, Italy, 49, **49**
Villiers, Janet and Geoffrey, 118
Virginia:
    Inn, The, 55–59, **55**, **58**
    Keswick Hall, 117, **117**
    L'Auberge Provencale, 59–64, **59**, **61**, **62**

Wald & Schlosshotel, Oehringen, Germany, 36–39
Wales:
    Llangoed Hall, 32, 33–36, **33**, **35**
Waterford, Ireland, 47
Wheatleigh, Berkshire Mountains, Massachusetts,
    43–47, **47**
White Barn Inn, The, Kennebunkport, Maine,
    12, **90**
White Horse Inn (Arundell Arms), 67
Williams, Brill, 86
Williams, Ione and Rodney, 86
William the Conqueror, 30
Wuthering Heights, 111
Wye River, Wales, 36